HIGH FIVE

DUKE'S Unforgettable 2015 Championship Season

Duke fans traveled to Indianapolis for the Final Four and showed their support during the Blue Devils' win over the Wisconsin Badgers in the title game.

Triumph Books LLC
814 North Franklin Street
Chicago, Illinois 60610
Phone: (312) 337-0747
www.triumphbooks.com

Printed in U.S.A.
ISBN: 978-1-62937-063-7

Content packaged by Mojo Media, Inc.
Joe Funk: Editor
Jason Hinman: Creative Director

Front and back cover photos by AP Images

Unless otherwise noted, all interior photos by AP Images

CONTENTS

APRIL 6, 2015 • INDIANAPOLIS, INDIANA
DUKE 68, WISCONSIN 63

ONE FOR THE THUMB

Freshmen Lead Second-Half Comeback as Duke, Coach K Capture Fifth Title

By Mike Lopresti

It ended just where the Duke Blue Devils wanted, and just how they wanted: All together on a podium in Indianapolis, watching One Shining Moment. Their One Shining Moment.

They stood there as new national champions, the final step taken with a difficult come-from-behind 68-63 win over Wisconsin. In the middle was Mike Krzyzewski. Next to him was senior Quinn Cook, the heart and soul of Duke, with tears running down his cheeks.

"He's been like a father to me over these last four years," Cook would say later. "To have his arm around me and hugging me while we're watching One Shining Moment was probably the best feeling of my life."

It was, indeed, a moment of deliverance for Duke.

For Cook who endured the March upsets by Lehigh and Mercer, and stayed long enough to lead a champion. "Surreal," he said. "It's been the best four years of my life, a true blessing. And dreams come true."

For four freshman, who had gone to Durham in a wave, intending for this very night to happen. When it was time to finish the job, they would score 60 of Duke's 68 points, and all 37 after halftime. Tyus Jones' 23 would lead the way and that earned him the Most Outstanding Player award. "I just wanted to be part of a special team," he said. "I just trusted Coach K and everyone on the staff with all my heart."

For Grayson Allen, the new folk hero of Durham. The least known of the four freshmen, he entered the title game with a four-point average. Eighteen games during the 2014-15 season, he did not score a point. But Allen put up 16 against Wisconsin, and with

Forward Justise Winslow drives to the basket during the NCAA title game matchup against Wisconsin.

Duke down nine in the second half, was a one-man life preserver with eight consecutive points and a steal.

"It doesn't feel real right now, to be honest," he said. "I saw them win in 2010, that national championship against Butler. I've dreamed about being in this moment since then. Never thought it would actually come true."

Said Krzyzewski, "We were dead in the water.... We won it because of that kid. We're not here without Grayson Allen."

And for Krzyzewski, now the most prolific men's national championship coach in history not named John Wooden. This was No. 5, but it was not the night for history. It was the night for the players grouped around him on that podium.

"He wasn't focused on getting his fifth championship. He was focused on getting our first," Cook said.

"The one you're in this moment, with it always the most current, you can feel it the best," Krzyzewski said. "I haven't loved a team any more than I've loved this team.

"We have eight guys and four of them are freshmen. For them to win 35 games and win the national title is incredible. When it's over—and I would have the best appreciation because I've been in this for 40 years—and I'm the coach of that group that did this, how good is that? They've been a joy. They've been an incredible joy. When you're already happy and you get happier, it's pretty damn good."

Quinn Cook maneuvers around Wisconsin's Nigel Hayes for a layup during the second half.

Jahlil Okafor gets past national player of the year Frank Kaminsky (44) to score two of his 10 points. Okafor was limited to 22 minutes due to foul trouble.

It was done basically with eight bodies who never ran out of purpose. "We said a couple of months ago, 'eight is enough,'" Krzyzewski said. "Eight is enough."

But why would the players believe eight was enough?

"Because," Jahlil Okafor said, "Coach K said it was."

Add complete trust on the list of Duke weapons that made this happen. Right there with the defense that allowed only 56.3 points and 38-percent shooting in the NCAA Tournament. And the offense that was forever trotting out a different nightly star. Duke won the title, and its most renowned player— Okafor—didn't even make the all-Final Four team. "We don't care who's scoring," Justise Winslow said. "We just care about Duke being up one at the end of the game."

Even all that nearly wasn't enough against Wisconsin. Fresh off ruining Kentucky's perfect season plans, the Badgers played Duke even in a first half of 13 lead changes, and eased ahead 48-39 with 13 minutes left. But Allen drained their momentum with his surge, and whatever Wisconsin had at the end could not stop Duke. Not even the 21 points and 12 rebounds of national player of the year Frank Kaminsky.

Jones' 3-pointer at 4:08 put Duke ahead to stay 59-58, though it was still only three points' difference in the final minute. The Blue Devils, fighting foul trouble to their bigs, hung on by refusing to yield baskets, or ground.

Duke players celebrate their 68-63 victory over Wisconsin. The championship marked the fifth national title for head coach Mike Krzyzewski in Coach K's 12th Final Four.

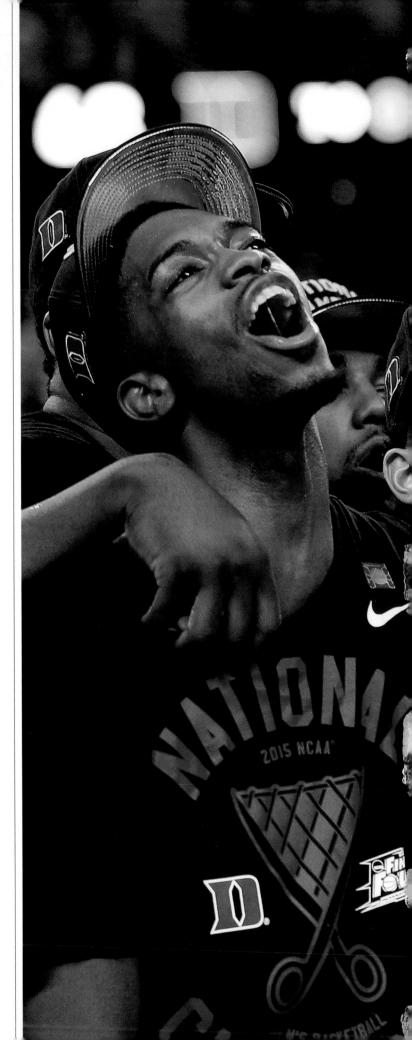

NATIONAL CHAMPIONS

NATIONAL CHAMPIONS

NCAA

2015
DIVISION I

MEN'S
BASKETBALL
CHAMPIONSHIP

NATIONAL CHAMPION

"How could there be a better way to win it than to play those last eight minutes with such grit and defense?" Krzyzewski said. "Our guys just fought and fought and fought. We had one of the smallest teams, I think, probably in the history of this championship on the floor. But not in heart."

The Badgers were left to mourn their 41 percent shooting, especially Sam Dekker and his 6-for-15 line. "I'm putting this one on me," Dekker said.

Wisconsin was also were less than happy with the officiating—Duke took and made 10 more free throws—and coach Bo Ryan was famously miffed at what he thought was a physical Blue Devils effort with too few whistles. Plus, a late out-of-bounds call that gave Duke the ball was incorrect. "I just feel sorry for my guys," he said. "It's just a shame that it had to be played that way."

When it was over, and Krzyzewski had gone 3-for-3 for titles in Indianapolis Final Fours, he made sure to pick up and hug each of his nine grandkids. At 68, he had just become the second oldest national champion coach ever, behind only Jim Calhoun.

But as he said many times, a team like this could make a man feel young again. ∎

Jahlil Okafor celebrates after teammate Tyus Jones nails a 3-pointer against Wisconsin. The two freshman combined for 33 points against the Badgers.

Coach K celebrates with his players at Lucas Oil Stadium following the win over Wisconsin. Three of the five titles Duke has won during Krzyzewski's tenure have happened in Indianapolis.

APRIL 4, 2015 • INDIANAPOLIS, INDIANA
DUKE 81, MICHIGAN STATE 61

BACK HOME AGAIN IN INDIANA

Blue Devils Crush Spartans

By Mike Lopresti

One more game.

Duke came to the Final Four, and nothing had changed from the first two impressive weeks of the NCAA Tournament. The defense was still resolute, the offense still efficient, the young guys still playing like veterans. Put all that together and the Blue Devils stormed more than advanced into the national championship game, crunching Michigan State 81-61.

Mike Krzyzewski was impressed, anyway.

"The lights and the stage have not been too big for them," he said. "They felt like they could sing their song and do their dance, and they've done it. They've done it really well."

Yep, Duke was back home again in Indiana.

Krzyzewski arrived with a 4-0 Final Four record in Indianapolis, and picked up where he left off in 2010. That early 14-6 Spartan lead? A mirage. After scoring 14 points the first 3:41, Michigan State managed to score 11 in the last 16:19 of the first half, missing 17 of 20 shots. Duke led 36-25 at halftime and never looked back.

"After the first four minutes," Krzyzewski said on a television interview, "we were a completely different team."

That meant lots of defense and lots of Justise Winslow, Jahlil Okafor, and Quinn Cook. They went for 19, 18, and 17 points, their combined 54 not far off the entire Spartans' production.

Michigan State, a No. 7 seed with 11 defeats, had barged into the Final Four as something of an underdog tale; another contender Tom Izzo pieced together just in time for March. But the Spartans had come to play the wrong team and the wrong coach

Quinn Cook goes up for a shot in the second half. Duke overcame an early Michigan State lead to secure the Final Four win, with senior Cook providing 17 of Duke's 81 points

in the wrong town for that sort of thing to continue. Krzyzewski was 8-1 against Izzo before the game, and 9-1 after it.

The Blue Devils dominated by shooting 52 percent and outscoring Michigan State from the line 27-10. It was the worst tournament drubbing in Michigan State history. Not that the numbers mattered much. What mattered was that Duke had pushed to the very doorknob of a national championship, and seemed to be getting harder to score against by the night. The Spartans were the first tournament opponent to break 60 against the Blue Devils, and not by much.

"Defense is what wins you games, especially in the postseason," Tyus Jones said. "We've known that since the beginning of the tournament."

Added Cook, "Week by week, I felt that guys were making tremendous strides on the defensive end."

Put that together with some crisp work on offense—Winslow, Okafor, and Cook were a combined 18-for-30 shooting, and the entire team had eight turnovers—and Duke seemed fully ready for one final bow.

"They really don't make a lot of mistakes," Michigan State's Branden Dawson said.

Krzyzewski paused to pay homage to his group. "Every night when I'm watching tape or I'm getting prepared, I never worry about attitude. I never worry that my guys aren't going to come," he said. "So you can be a little bit more creative.

Guard Tyus Jones, who played 38 minutes of the Final Four win over Michigan State, dribbles past Michigan State's Lourawls Nairn Jr.

Jahlil Okafor slams two points home during the first half against the Spartans. The freshman big man scored 18 points in 30 minutes.

"It's not a little exciting. It's incredibly exciting. Now they've got a chance to play for the national championship. Damn, how exciting is that?"

So Krzyzewski would be wearing his championship ring from 2010 for two more days. He had it on all month, "as a reminder" of where the Blue Devils were trying to go.

"We had one goal when the year began. We're going to try to make that happen," Tyus Jones said. "This is why we came here. For it to be right in front of us, 40 minutes away, means everything."

One more game. ■

Above: Duke sophomore Jack Grady, watching the game at Cameron Indoor Stadium, celebrates during the Final Four win over Michigan State. Right: Jahlil Okafor, Duke's second leading scorer behind Justise Winslow, drives to the basket during the first half.

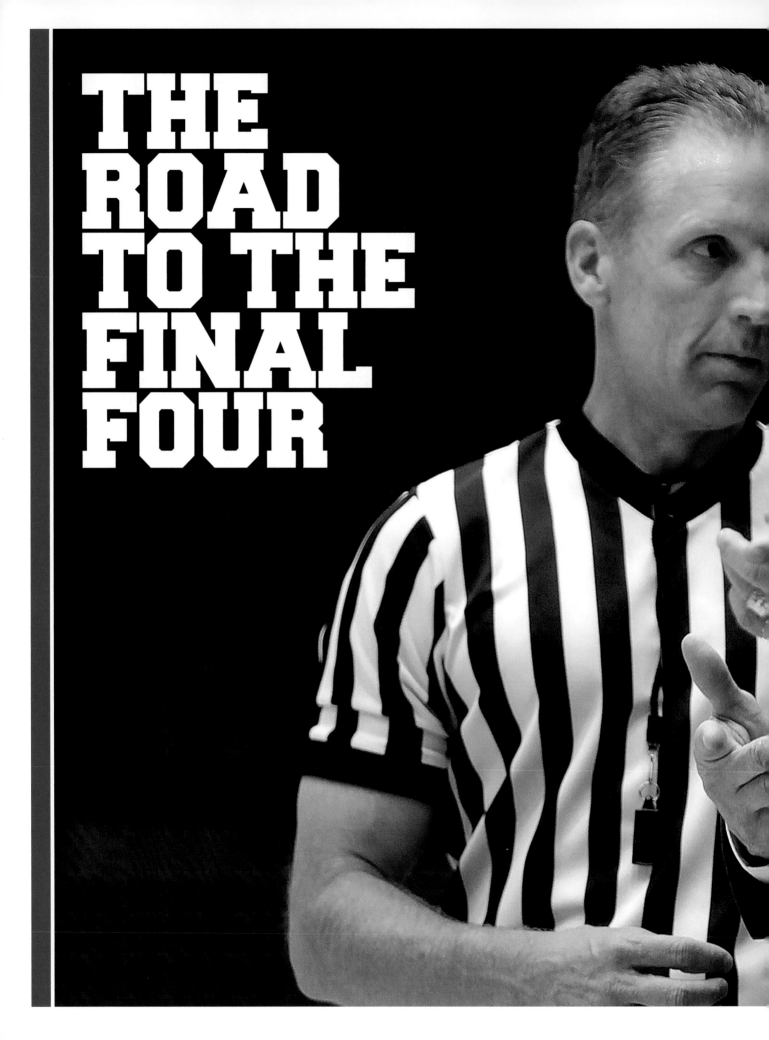

THE ROAD TO THE FINAL FOUR

Mike Krzyzewski argues with official Mike Eades during a Nov. 8 exhibition game against Central Missouri at Cameron Indoor Stadium. Duke won 87-47.

NOVEMBER 18, 2014 • INDIANAPOLIS, INDIANA
DUKE 81, MICHIGAN STATE 71

FRESHMEN PASS FIRST TEST

Blue Devils Top Spartans in Champions Classic

By Matt Silverman

There is a reason they call it the Champions Classic. Four schools—Duke, Kentucky, Michigan State, and Kansas—committed to play each November on a rotating basis. Three of the four teams would reach the Final Four in March of 2015.

The first Champions Classic was held at Madison Square Garden in 2011 and Duke beat Michigan State by five. The next year the Blue Devils beat Kentucky by seven at the Georgia Dome. Duke lost in the Champions Classic for the first time in 2013, falling to Kansas by 11 at the United Center in Chicago. The series was extended for a new three-year rotation in 2014, starting at the Bankers Life Fieldhouse in Indianapolis.

The USA Today Preseason Coaches Poll had three teams from the Champions Classic field in its top five: Kentucky (No. 1), Duke (No. 3), and Kansas (No. 5). Michigan State was the outlier, just barely in the top 20, but like Duke, MSU came into the Classic undefeated. Duke had whipped Presbyterian and Fairfield by an average of almost 60 points in Durham, marking the first time since 1997-98 that the Blue Devils reached triple digits in consecutive games. Michigan State, which won its first game of the year in a much closer contest against Navy, would be the first real taste of big-time college basketball for Duke's newcomers.

Indianapolis was where both teams wanted to finish the season, although the exact location was a half mile southwest: Lucas Oil Stadium, where the 2014-15 Final Four would be held. And Indianapolis was where the real work began toward that goal. Banker's

Justise Winslow drives to the basket as Spartans forward Matt Costello defends. The freshman forward scored 15 points in Duke's Champions Classic win over Michigan State.

Life Fieldhouse, home to the NBA's Indiana Pacers, would also be the first college road trip for Duke's trio of fantastic freshmen: Jahlil Okafor, Justise Winslow, and Tyus Jones. They looked like seasoned pros.

Facing the defending Big Ten champs, Duke took the floor with the three freshmen and both captains, senior Quinn Cook and junior Amile Jefferson. It marked the first time since 1983 that freshmen started consecutive games for Duke. That mark would soon fall, as did every shot the Blue Devils put up in the opening minutes. Duke hit its first seven shots and went up by 10 about midway through the first half. Duke took a 40-33 lead into intermission on 56 percent shooting against one of the top defensive teams in the country. Winslow, Okafor, and Cook netted 10 points apiece in the first half.

But Tom Izzo never quits, even if the Michigan State coach had been enviously watching the Chicago-born Okafor since eighth grade. It was just a matter of which school he would be playing for, and who he'd be playing with. The freshman trio accounted for 49 points, with Jones and Okafor scoring 17 apiece, while Cook led all scorers with 19 and had six assists. Okafor missed only two shots, making him 25 of 30 to open his Duke career.

The Spartans cut the deficit to 51-48 with 13:54 left in the game, but MSU never got any closer and never led. Duke's speed and athleticism proved too much, resulting in plenty of mistakes by Michigan State, which was outscored on turnovers, 24-4.

Guard Tyus Jones scores two of his 17 points against Michigan State. Duke's three freshman starters combined for 49 of Duke's 81 points in the win.

Mike Krzyzewski, who assembled this crew after losing seven players from the year before—four to graduation, two to the NBA draft, and one to transfer—was pleased to see how the team reacted to its first test. "I thought we handled it well," Krzyzewski said after the 81-71 win, Duke's largest margin of victory yet in a Champions Classic and the team's fourth straight against Michigan State.

It would not be the last time these two played during the season—and it wouldn't be the last time they met in Indianapolis, either. Albeit at the bigger building just a 10-minute walk down the street, with a lot more riding on the outcome. ∎

Above: Jahlil Okafor drives in for a layup during the third regular season game of his Duke career. Okafor converted on eight of 10 field goal attempts. Right: Tyus Jones puts up a shot during the second half.

HEAD COACH

MIKE KRZYZEWSKI

Legendary Coach Wins by Understanding How to Change
By Mike Lopresti

In the end, this would be the great irony about Mike Krzyzewski.

He is a 68-year-old man with 1,018 wins, and a gaggle of grandchildren. You could tell by all the kids he had to pick up and hug on the court at Lucas Oil Stadium after the national championship game in Indianapolis. And you know the cliché about senior citizens; how they can be a little stuck in their ways.

But here he was with a fifth championship, largely because he knew how to change. An aging legend still going strong, because he understood how to be new.

"The ability to adapt is key in everything," he said. "I think I've adapted well."

If he had to alter his style, he would. If he had to tweak his strategy, he would. If he needed to bring talented freshmen into the Duke family atmosphere, knowing they would likely be one and gone—call him Mike Calipari—he would. He would be stubborn about not being stubborn.

And it would all work.

"With guys who aren't going to be here as long," he said, "what we've tried to do over the last few years is get to know them even better, before they got to Duke."

Which is why, on the night the Blue Devils won the national championship, they sounded as if they had been together forever on a desert island, not just one winter in Durham. "He has been our rock," Jahlil Okafor said of Krzyzewski. "I believed in everything that they told me," Tyus Jones said.

Krzyzewski did another important thing, as the modern man. He kept his players in the moment. Their moment.

"All year, he has been making it not about his fifth championship, but our first together," Quinn Cook said. "I can remember when we won the 1,000th game for him, he was more worried about us getting our 17th win."

Coach Mike Krzyzewski cuts down the net following Duke's win over Wisconsin in the NCAA title game. The win was the culmination of an amazing season for the 68-year-old head coach, who also collected his 1,000th career win in January.

Indeed, it was usually as hard to get Krzyzewski to look backward during the NCAA Tournament as it was to score against his defense.

"I don't like to bring up what's been done in the past, whether we've won or we've lost, because we've already done that," he said. "It's what you're doing right now, and how emotionally and mentally ready you can be for your team."

Curious thing, that a man who understands so well how to keep the past in perspective just keeps adding treasure to it.

It is how Krzyzewski could thrive so long in a merciless profession, that on January 25, he would be the first men's coach to crack the 1,000-win barrier. Even fate played along, allowing it to happen on such a hallowed stage as Madison Square Garden. Krzyzewski said that day he was lucky and honored. And also he was glad it was over, there was a season to get to.

It is how he has now gone to Final Fours in four different decades, and won championships in three of them. During his stay at Duke, Kentucky has seen six coaches, and the White House has seen six presidents.

It is why he has been such a gold medal machine as coach of Team USA, helping restore American basketball to power, as he did at Duke. A coach doesn't mesh NBA players so well without being flexible.

And it is why, as his Blue Devils relentlessly plowed together toward the championship, he seemed to only look spryer.

"I still have the desire to prepare to win, and want to win," he said one day. "But along

Coach K celebrates with players and fans during a homecoming event on April 7 at Cameron Indoor Stadium, the day after Duke defeated Wisconsin to capture the school's fifth national championship.

with that I have a responsibility to have the drive for the players that I have the privilege to coach. I shouldn't coach unless I have the drive, and you can't fake it.

"For me, it's always come easy to have drive. Sometimes I haven't been the smartest guy or whatever, but the passion to win has never been a thing I've run out of yet."

He had it when Duke hired him from Army in the spring of 1980. The Associated Press story that day made a point of spelling his name phonetically, kre-ches-skee. Good idea. But wrong.

He had it when Duke went 38-47 his first three years, and people started to wonder. He had it when the Blue Devils fell short of the title his first four trips to the Final Four.

He had it the recent puzzling years, when Duke was quickly escorted out of the tournament by Lehigh and Mercer.

And he certainly had it with this team of short numbers but unshakable purpose. A Few Good Men.

"There hasn't been a practice or game where I can say Coach wasn't there that day," Cook said at the Final Four. "He brings it every day, every game, and for a guy with four national championships to have that drive and hunger, it shows why he's one of the greats. He instills that drive into his players."

Krzyzewski had said how, "I still try to approach everything like I'm coach at Army. I think that's what my players deserve. They deserve you to be hungry and prepared."

This team apparently made that easy for him.

During some of the tense moments of the Wisconsin title game, Krzyzewki's daughter

Mike Krzyzewski sits on the court during the second half of the NCAA title game against Wisconsin. Krzyzewski's game plan was key as the Blue Devils overcame a nine-point deficit in the second half to defeat the Badgers.

Lindy was walking the concourse of Lucas Oil Stadium, too nervous to watch. She understood how badly her father wanted this championship, for this team.

"He's been so happy. You know, usually he's got that scowl on his face," she said later, with the title secured. "You didn't see any of that. He loved these boys and they loved one another. They were on a mission."

But he's usually happy coaching, right?

"Not like this year," she said. "This year is different."

By midnight April 6, Mike Krzyzewski was one championship older. As a coach, he had never looked younger. ■

Above: Never shy to share his feelings about a questionable call, Mike Krzyzewski reacts during Duke's Jan. 3 win over Boston College. Right: Krzyzewski argues with an official during the second half of Duke's Dec. 15 win over Elon.

DECEMBER 3, 2014 • MADISON, WISCONSIN

DUKE 80, WISCONSIN 70

WINNING IN HOSTILE TERRITORY

Freshmen Lead Blue Devils to Defining Win Over No. 2 Badgers

By Matt Silverman

After winning their first seven games by an average margin of 31 points, Duke faced its most difficult task of the young season—and its first true road game. Duke had played in the Championship Classic in Indianapolis and the Coaches vs. Cancer Classic at the Barclays Center in Brooklyn, but those were neutral site games, which for a school with a fanatical national following like Duke means a lot of blue shirts in the stands. The December game against Wisconsin not only pitted the fourth-ranked Blue Devils against a team ranked two spots ahead of them in the USA Today Men's Basketball Coaches Poll, this game also brought the young Duke team into hostile territory: Madison's Kohl Center.

Heading into the season, Duke coach Mike Krzyzewski said he thought Wisconsin was the best team in the country. Now he would get to see first hand how accurate this assessment was.

Bo Ryan's Badgers were renowned through the years for tenacious defense, but Wisconsin had added a high-powered offensive component that transformed the school from the team no one wanted to play to national championship contender. In March of 2014, Wisconsin reached the Final Four for just the second time since 1941 with a one-point win over Arizona. The Badgers missed reaching the finals by one point against Kentucky. Wisconsin graduated point guard Ben Brust, but they still had seniors Frank Kaminsky, Josh Gasser and Traveon Jackson, plus junior standout Sam Dekker and sophomore forward Nigel Hayes. Duke also faced a Kohl Center

Quinn Cook drives to the basket as Wisconsin's Josh Gasser defends during the first half.

crowd intent on showing the ESPN audience that the Cameron Center wasn't the only venue that could get crazy.

Two top five-ranked teams, both undefeated, giving an early December basketball game an early April feel. This was exactly why the ACC/Big Ten Challenge was created.

Both teams were up for the challenge. Wisconsin took a four-point early in the game, but the freshmen they'd been hearing so much about in Madison and, well, everywhere else, slowly took over the game. Or quickly, if you watched them move around the floor.

Duke confounded Wisconsin's offense by switching defenses, the ensuing mismatches created problems for the flow of Wisconsin's regular offense as the Badgers tried to adjust on the fly to what seemed like an advantage. The advantage often wound up turning into Duke's. The Blue Devils limited Wisconsin to just nine field goals in the second half and held the Badgers to 40.7 percent from the field in the game. With Duke shooting 65 percent for the game—and 71 percent in the second half—the Blue Devils racked up 80 points, the most allowed by Wisconsin all year.

Tyus Jones, whose family drove nearly five hours from Minneapolis, made the trip worthwhile, scoring 22 points on 7-of-11 shooting from the field and hitting 2 of 3 from beyond the three-point line. Months later, Jones would still call it his best game. Playing in front of familiar faces in a sea of red also helped bolster that view. "You know, seeing

Duke's Marshall Plumlee dunks during the first half. The senior contributed four points in eight minutes.

my mom right behind the bench...helps and she was loving it," he said.

Duke had few better nights during the season. The Blue Devils had confounded and contained one of the best teams in the country in just the eighth college game for Duke's talented freshmen. Jahlil Okafor (13 points) did not give up too much against Frank Kaminsky (17 points), who would be the Associated Press Player of the Year; Tyus Jones' speed helped open up a tight game in the final three minutes with a layup plus an assist on an Amile Jefferson jumper to make it 69-60; and Justise Winslow's dunk off an inbounds pass knocked the air out of any thoughts of a Wisconsin comeback with 1:23 remaining. "They didn't look like freshmen tonight," Krzyzewski said.

Wisconsin's Traevon Jackson, who led all scorers with 25 points, was prophetic in his observation. "It was a great test and a great Duke team," he said. "And the biggest thing is just to make sure it doesn't happen again."

Four months later, when these teams prepared to meet again with much more at stake, Mike Krzyzewski recalled how impressive the game in Madison was and how unfazed his freshmen were going into an unfriendly environment and taking on a team as accomplished as Wisconsin. "I mean, you can't teach that," he said of the December 3 game. "They had it. Win or lose, I was going to come away from that game knowing that this would be a team that wouldn't be afraid of the bright lights and the big stage." ■

Tyus Jones shares a moment with fans behind Duke's bench following Duke's 80-70 win at Wisconsin on Dec. 3. The game represented a homecoming for Jones, whose family drove nearly five hours from Minneapolis to Madison to attend the game.

15

<u>CENTER</u>

JAHLIL OKAFOR

Top Recruit Makes Most of Only College Season

By Matt Silverman

If a player is going to do the proverbial "one and done" from college to the NBA, it's hard to imagine it being done any better than Jahlil Okafor: from Chicago's Whitney Young High School to Duke University to NBA lottery pick. Throw in a national championship and that certainly makes for quite a year.

Before he even played his first game at Duke, the honors Okafor had received by age 18 staggered the mind, not to mention the trophy case: McDonald's All-American, McDonald All-American Game MVP, unanimous No. 1 prospect in his class by ESPN and most other outlets, Parade and USA Today Player of the Year, 2014 Morgan Wootten National High School Player of the Year, 2014 Mr. Basketball in Illinois, and all-state in Illinois two or three times, depending on which Chicago paper you prefer—the

Tribune (two) or *Sun-Times* (three). Plus myriad other awards to take up pages in NBA media guides for years to come. Chicago native Mike Krzyzewski wasn't just interested in him because they share the same hometown.

Krzyzewski told Sports Illustrated that his top three selections to come to Duke in the fall of 2014 were Tyus Jones, Justise Winslow, and Okafor—no surprise. But it was a bit of a shock when he said the school had no backup plan in place. "The guilt trip that sometimes people put these kids through, I don't want that to be the basis of our relationship," he said. "We didn't recruit some other kid because we wanted to show them: You're the guy we want. I want them to trust me from the very beginning."

Okafor and Jones, who became friends through USA Basketball, grew even closer during a competition in Lithuania. They made a pact to attend the same college. At 6-foot-11, agile,

Jahlil Okafor celebrates a dunk during Duke's win at Louisville on Jan. 17. Okafor scored 18 points in the win, which ended Duke's two-game losing streak.

and with hands so big they make the basketball look small, Okafor is the kind of specimen that coaches, scouts, and fans drool over. Given the national attention and countless college offers he received, his father, Chukwundi Okafor—Jahlil's mother died when he was in third grade—invited five schools to visit: Baylor, Kansas, Michigan State, Ohio State, and Duke. The decision was carried on ESPNU with the two friends in different gyms in different states, but putting on the same color hat at the same time. Justise Winslow, who had also played with them for USA Basketball, committed to Duke a week later.

Had they decided to go somewhere else, Duke would have been like the kid left out in musical chairs. It being Duke—and with Krzyzewski being coach of the Olympic team—the program probably would have figured something out, but the Blue Devils probably would not have been cutting down the nets in Indianapolis in 2015.

At Duke, the big man was as good as advertised. Okafor averaged 17.3 points and 8.5 rebounds in what—to few people's surprise—would be his only year in college before he declared for the NBA draft. Krzyzewski even said as much before his first game with the Blue Devils. "We won't have him long," he told reporters.

Jahlil Okafor finds his way to the basket during the second half of Duke's 70-59 win over Stanford during the Coaches vs. Cancer Classic at Brooklyn's Barclays Center.

The honors kept coming for Okafor. He won awards before the season even began, including Preseason All-American and Preseason ACC Rookie of the Year, both of which proved prescient since he won those awards after the season as well. He even won the ACC Player of the Year Award after finishing second to Marcus Paige of North Carolina in the preseason voting. Okafor was the first freshman to receive the award.

While playing 30 minutes per game for Duke, he shot 66.4 percent from the field. His foul shooting remained an area in need of work, though. He shot just 51 percent from the line at Duke after hitting 57 percent in high school.

He scored a season high of 30 points in an overtime win in February against Virginia Tech after sitting out the previous game with an ankle injury. More impressive was the 28 points he scored in a semifinal loss to Notre Dame in the ACC tournament. Before the game, Krzyzewski spoke to him about playing better to help his teammates. He responded with a monster game. Duke was down for much of the contest, but the Blue Devils made a late run at the Fighting Irish. It probably would not have been close without Okafor's effort. Despite losing, the experience was the ideal preparation for the NCAA tournament.

Jahlil Okafor rejects a shot by Boston College's Patrick Heckmann during the Blue Devils' win over the Golden Eagles on Jan. 3.

JAHLIL OKAFOR

When asked after the national championship game why he thought that Krzyzewski's eight-man rotation involved enough players, he answered, "Because Coach K said it was. That is how great he is and when he says something you believe it. He tells us we are going to win and we believe it. He has been our rock all year."

Okafor battled Wisconsin's "tank," Frank Kaminsky, also 6-foot-11 and the National Player of the Year, for the 2015 NCAA tournament title. Okafor made a couple of key baskets in the closing minutes, finishing with 10 points.

Unlike the outcome of the championship game, or even his choice on where to attend college, his decision to leave after a year for the NBA was no surprise. He joined Corey Maggette (1999), Luol Deng (2004), Kyrie Irving (2011), Austin Rivers (2012), and Jabari Parker (2014)—not to mention his friend Justise Winslow—as Duke freshmen entering the NBA draft after one year with the Blue Devils. His coach applauded the decision and said, "He will always be a part of our Duke basketball family." And he will always be crucial part of Coach K's fifth national championship. ◼

Jahlil Okafor maneuvers around Wisconsin's Frank Kaminsky during the NCAA title game. Both players were first-team All-Americans.

JANUARY 25, 2015 • NEW YORK CITY
DUKE 77, ST. JOHN'S 68

COACH 1K

Second-Half Comeback Seals Krzyzewski's 1,000th Career Win
By Matt Silverman

The list of victims includes schedule fillers and Cinderellas, dynasties and doormats. Add them all up, insert the number of times coached against each one, subtract the losses, and you'd get 1,000. Or 999, to be exact.

No coach in Division I history had ever approached four digits worth of wins. E.A. Diddle of Western Kentucky achieved 759 wins in 1964. He was soon passed by Adolph Rupp (876) of Kentucky. Dean Smith (879) topped Rupp. Then Bobby Knight passed Smith in his last full season and retired midway through the 2007-08 season with 902 career wins.

By the time Knight left Texas Tech, he was being pursued by someone he knew quite well: Mike Krzyzewski. A former captain under Knight at Army and then a captain in the U.S. Army, the Chicago-born Krzyzewski coached service teams and spent two years as coach at the U.S. Military Academy Prep School in Virginia. He left the service and was graduate assistant to Knight at Indiana before returning to Army as head coach at age 28. His first win came in 1975 against Lehigh. Duke hired him in 1980 when Bill Foster left for South Carolina. Duke was a top notch program, and Krzyzewski was coming off a 9-17 season at Army, still his fewest wins and lowest winning percentage (.346) of any full season as a head coach.

Duke failed to reach the NCAA tournament in his first three years. Since then, beginning in 1984 he has reached the NCAAs every year save one—1995, when Coach K missed most of the year following back surgery. He won national championships in 1991, 1992, 2001, and 2010, and the wins kept adding up. So by 2015, as the odometer was about to crack 1,000, where would the schedule have Krzyzewski that day? Not Durham, not another ACC outpost, not even Chapel Hill, but in New York City.

Jahlil Okafor shoots over St. John's forward Chris Obekpa during the second half of Duke's Jan. 25 win over St. John's. Okafor had 17 points and 10 rebounds in coach Mike Krzyzewski's 1,000th career win.

Of course, he had coached in New York many times. Before he was Coach K to the world, when he was just a guy with a hard name to pronounce coaching at a military academy, he took his 1977 Army team to Alumni Hall in Queens and lost by 13 to Lou Carnesecca and the St. John's Redmen (as they were then known). Madison Square Garden—and life as coach at Duke—proved kinder in terms of results.

Madison Square Garden was where Krzyzewski passed his college coach and mentor, Bobby Knight, with win number 903—a neutral court game in the 2011 Big Apple Preseason NIT against Michigan State. St. John's and Duke have played each other most years since 1999, alternating home court for midwinter contests, right in the middle of the conference season—a break from the usual suspects, but a loss could hurt a team's designs to gain momentum heading into tournament season. Duke's momentum was usually fine, St. John's was often the one worse for wear. Krzyzewski's record at the Garden with Duke stood at 25-8, 15-2 against St. John's.

But none of that mattered to the 2015 Red Storm. Coach Steve Lavin—like many St. John's coaches before him—sought a résumé-building win with March in mind. On a Sunday afternoon at the Garden in front of a national audience, the 13-5 Red Storm fell behind early—as expected—but they came roaring back, erasing an 11-point deficit to take a 43-39 halftime lead over the Blue Devils, just the second time the team had

Following the win over St. John's, Duke players donned t-shirts celebrating their coach's milestone achievement.

trailed after 20 minutes all year. There were many fans in blue as well as former Duke alums and players at MSG, and those who had come to see a celebration were getting a ballgame.

St. John's pushed its lead to 10 early in the second half and it was still up by double digits with 8:35 remaining. Duke was still working on defense, not allowing a single 3-point basket in the second half. That was partly due to the zone defense, introduced following successive losses to North Carolina State and Miami. It was a departure for a program that had been staunchly man-to-man since basketball shorts were actually short. But a coach doesn't become the first to approach 1,000 wins by being obstinate or by ignoring recruits who might want to play both at Duke and in the NBA before they turn 20.

St. John's didn't get a single point from their bench, while Duke received 10 points and significant minutes from Matt Jones, Grayson Allen, and Rasheed Sulaimon. With the Red Storm in foul trouble, the Blue Devils outscored them 26-7 down the stretch; freshman Tyus Jones (22 points) finishing the comeback with 10-for-10 foul shooting. The 77-68 victory was a present to their coach as well as a gift to those close to him who wouldn't have to pack up to go to South Bend to see Coach K take another whack at 1,000. Now they could celebrate.

"We want to celebrate this with each other," Jahlil Okafor (17 points, 10 rebounds) said after the game. "It seemed like he was enjoying it for us because we were able to be a part of it. Everyone who helped him get to this point including the staff at Army and the staff here at Duke."

"To win the 1,000th here, you need to be a lucky guy," said the coach of the hour, or, given all the "1 K" signs at the Garden, coach of the millennium might be more appropriate. "I like my place, Cameron, but this is a magical place and we beat a really good team and a storied program. A storied program that I've had respect for since I was a player at Army a long time ago, about 48, 49 years ago. Their program has stood the test of time and so has ours."

"It was great to do it in the same place he got 903," Okafor said of Madison Square Garden, "and that was something I watched on TV, so it's sort of surreal to think I am here right now."

Coach K thanked everyone, basked in the glow for a moment, and was about as honest as a man who has averaged more than 25 wins a year for four decades could be about passing another milestone: "I'm glad it's over!" ∎

Tyus Jones shoots a 3-pointer during the second half of Duke's win over St. John's. The freshman guard was the game's leading scorer with 22 points, including two 3-pointers.

12 FORWARD

JUSTISE WINSLOW

Nothing "Small" About Talented Freshman

By Matt Silverman

At 6-foot-6 and 229 pounds, Justise Winslow stretches the definition of the term "small forward." But the multitalented Texan played a big role in Duke becoming national champions for the fifth time. He will head for the NBA after just one season as a Blue Devil, but he leaves a legacy is as being part of one of college basketball's most successful freshman trios.

Winslow was not part of the pact formed by Tyus Jones and Jahlil Okafor to attend the same school, but Winslow played with them and considered them good friends. Raised in Houston, Winslow joined Jones and Okafor, both Midwesterners, for the 2012 Under-17 Championships. They finished first. The next year Winslow and Okafor were the only two high schoolers on a team that won the gold medal in the under-19 category. Being the youngest—but far from the smallest—members of a team full of college and soon-to-be NBA players didn't hurt either player's development.

Winslow's final choice of schools—UCLA, Arizona, Florida, and Texas A&M—were altogether different than Jones or Okafor's picks, except for one. Announcing his decision one week after Jones and Okafor, Winslow too told the world he would play at Duke.

"It's a little early to talk about a national championship," he said when he committed in 2013. But it's fine to talk about it now.

The trio's familiarity with each other from their shared experiences in the International Basketball Federation (FIBA)—and the fact that Mike Krzyzewski heads USA Basketball—no doubt worked in Duke's favor. There is nothing wrong with the connection, it is a benefit of the decade spent by Krzyzewski building up a program that was being outclassed internationally but now outclasses the world.

Justise Winslow drives to the basket against N.C. State on Jan. 11. The multitalented freshman forward from Texas provided versatility on both ends of the floor that was integral to Duke's success.

As for Duke, adding three McDonald's All-Americans who had already played together, plus a fourth—Grayson Allen—put all the pieces in place for a legendary freshman class at Duke. After the Blue Devils were bounced from the 2014 NCAA tournament in the first round, falling to 14th-seeded Mercer in Raleigh, the talk in Durham about a national championship in 2015 began in earnest.

The season previews called Winslow "versatile," and that flexibility made him even more integral to Duke's attack. His superb ball skills aided the team's physicality and to help beat tough zone defenses. He also played a key part in Duke's adapting a zone defense after the team hit a lull in January and lost consecutive games to North Carolina State and Miami following 14 wins in a row out of the box. When Okafor rolled his ankle and had to miss the Clemson game, Winslow's versatility allowed him to move from small forward to power forward, making one of the top teams in the country even more dangerous. Winslow responded by shooting 57 percent from the field after the switch, and 53 percent from the arc. Sports Illustrated referred to his "relentless energy" and being "too quick for bigger players to guard." His pal Okafor called him "a man-child." Following Duke's ouster from the ACC tournament in the semifinals, the Blue Devils were ready to

Justise Winslow goes up for a dunk during Duke's Feb. 28 home win over Syracuse.

take on all comers in the NCAA tournament.

Despite their inexperience on paper, the freshmen—plus senior captain Quinn Cook, talented sophomore Matt Jones, and junior big men Amile Jefferson and Marshall Plumlee—were not about to be knocked out in the first round in 2015. As the No. 1 seed in the South, the Blue Devils plowed through Robert Morris and San Diego State. Utah was a tougher challenge, but Winslow played 37 minutes and poured in 21 points and grabbed 10 rebounds in a six-point win in the Sweet Sixteen. After pushing past Gonzaga to get to the Final Four, Duke faced Michigan State for the second time. Winslow had scored 15 points with five assists in a 10-point victory over the Spartans in November in the Champions Classic in Indianapolis at the Bankers Life Fieldhouse; now they matched up again in Indianapolis, this time at Lucas Oil Stadium. Duke won by 20 as Winslow scored 19. His NCAA tournament scoring average of 14.3 points and 9.3 rebounds was higher than his average during the season.

In the championship game against Wisconsin—another team Duke defeated early in the season—the Blue Devils fell behind and Winslow found himself on the bench in foul trouble, as did Okafor. Winslow scored 11 and grabbed nine rebounds with the title on the line, but whether or not his foot touched the

Justise Winslow finds his way to the basket during Duke's Feb. 9 win at Florida State.

out-of-bounds line ended up being a major topic of conversation. Driving to the baseline with three minutes to play and Duke up by a point, Winslow appeared to step on the line, but the officials did not call it. Winslow dished it to Okafor for the bucket. That set the stage for Winslow's next appendage controversy.

With Duke up by five and after a missed shot by the Badgers, the ball appeared to graze Winslow's fingertips. Again, the call went Duke's way. The Blue Devils won by six.

It was unfortunate that questions about calls had such a prominent part in the late stages of the game, somewhat overshadowing Duke's comeback from a nine-point deficit with 13:23 left. It was a great comeback, and a great season. Winslow's only season in Durham. The skills that made him so versatile—and so valuable—at Duke, promised to reward him at the pro level. His Duke tenure was brief, but his legacy was as a driving force on a national championship team: versatile, powerful, unstoppable, and nothing small about it. ■

Justise Winslow battles Wisconsin's Bronson Koenig during the second half of the NCAA title game. Winslow elevated his game in the NCAA tournament, averaging 14.3 points and 9.3 rebounds.

JANUARY 31, 2015 • CHARLOTTESVILLE, VIRGINIA
DUKE 69, VIRGINIA 63

COOK FOR THE COMEBACK

Duke Shreds Virginia Defense, Scores 43 in Second Half

By Mike Lopresti

Duke was done, of course.

No. 2 Virginia was ahead 58-50 with under five minutes left, and the Cavaliers were 19-0 on the season and had won 21 in a row at home and nobody had shot 50 percent against them in 43 consecutive games. Especially the Blue Devils, who had missed their first nine 3-point attempts of the night.

So No. 4 Duke was done. No rational reason to expect a comeback, right? Wrong.

Quinn Cook hit a 3-pointer, and Jahlil Okafor scored on a tip-in and then Cook hit another 3-point and then Matt Jones hit one, and then Cook hit another, and Tyus Jones added one, too. By then, it was Virginia that was done, the Blue Devils winning 69-63 in the biggest five-minute fireworks display this side of Disney World.

The Duke team that made one 3-pointer in the first 35 minutes hit five in the last 4:41. Nobody shreds the Virginia defense like that, but Duke just had. The Cavaliers came in allowing 49 points a game. The Blue Devils scored 43 in the second half.

"It is weird losing this way," Virginia guard Justin Anderson said. "Because that is who we are."

But on the last day of January, this is who the Blue Devils were:

They finished a week that began with Krzyzewski's 1,000th win, in Madison Square Garden against St. John's. And wasn't that a big to-do. Then came a loss at Notre Dame when the Blue Devils blew a 10-point lead in the last 10½ minutes. Then the dismissal of Rasheed Sulaimon the next day, the first time Krzyzewski had ever booted a Duke player.

Justise Winslow looks for his shot against a smothering Virginia defense. Winslow had 15 points and 11 rebounds in the win over No. 2 Virginia, ending the Cavaliers' 21-game home winning streak.

And finally, a visit to Virginia, which had been a dark tunnel for anyone else lately. Not since 1982—the days of Ralph Sampson and the infancy of Krzyzewski's Duke career—had these two met in Charlottesville as top-five ranked teams.

"It's been a hell of a week," Krzyzewski said.

But it certainly ended well, with 17 points from Jones and 15 each from Cook and Justise Winslow. Winslow also had 11 rebounds, for his first double-double as a Blue Devil. Duke shot nearly 51 percent and had only eight turnovers. By the end, the Blue Devils had scored 20 points above Virginia's defensive average. The 11-point Cavalier lead with 10 minutes to go turned out just an inconvenience.

"We're a resilient team," Oakfor said. "When we have our backs against the all, we respond."

But how did they pull this out of the hat in such a hostile, dangerous place?

"Belief," Jones said.

Especially on the road. The win gave the Blue Devils victories at Wisconsin, Louisville and Virginia. Those three were a combined 40-2 when Duke visited. That seemed a big hint of something special.

"We've shown it before, being tough" Krzyzewski said. "But in order to beat this team (Virginia), you have to take it up a notch.

"We have the potential to be very good. But we're not there yet."

But clearly, they were on their way. ∎

Jahlil Okafor puts up a shot against Virginia. Okafor contributed 10 points to the win, including a key tip-in in the game's final minutes.

5 GUARD

TYUS JONES

Duke's Smallest Player Came Up Big in Title Game
By Matt Silverman

Credentials were not lacking for the 2014-15 freshman class at Duke. The team boasted four McDonald's All-Americans fresh out of high school: one was the big man, Jahlil Okafor; one the versatile forward who makes scouts drool and opponents frustrated, Justise Winslow; another was the surprise slam dunk champion from the McDonald's All-American game who came up huge with the national championship on the line, Grayson Allen; but the one who set them up—and could knock it down too—was Tyus Jones. He was the driving force.

Minutes after helping Duke win the national championship, scoring a game-high 23 points, and making all seven free throw attempts in the 68-63 win over Wisconsin, Jones was asked what brought him from halfway across the country to Duke. "I just wanted to be a part of a special team," said the Minnesota-born Jones, whose only road game within driving distance for his family was at Wisconsin in December. "I knew the guys on the team already prior to stepping on campus. I knew Grayson, Justise, and Jah even before we got to campus. I just trusted Coach K and everyone on the staff with all my heart. I believed in everything that they told me. I just wanted to help, you know, contribute to such a special group."

Coach Mike Krzyzewski had his own compliments for his smallest player at 6-foot-1, but the one he'd entrusted the keys to a high-powered machine. "He's good. You start out with that," he said. "One of the reasons we waited three years to get him is because I thought he had special qualities, not just special talents. It shows up in big games and big moments."

He even came with his own frontcourt.

Tyus Jones celebrates after hitting a crucial 3-pointer in Duke's win over Wisconsin in the NCAA title game. Jones was the game's leading scorer with 23 points.

Okafor, from Chicago, had been a friend for almost a decade as both players attended USA Basketball Camps. They grew even closer thanks to the many games and road trips over summers competing at a national level. Okafor and Jones made a pact to attend the same college, even orchestrating an ESPNU selection show televised from two different locations. Duke was the choice—as it was for another former USA Basketball teammate, Justis Winslow. These three, plus Grayson Allen, formed a freshman nucleus on a team with only one senior, Quinn Cook. The cupboard was far from bare, though. Sophomore Matt Jones (no relation), got better and better as he was given more responsibility, plus junior big men Amile Jefferson and Marshall Plumlee added presence inside.

The Blue Devils were off and running, tearing through the first two months of the season without a loss. Jones scored 22 in the showdown with Wisconsin, where he was thrilled to have his mother sitting behind the Duke bench. He scored 21 in a victory over defending national champion Connecticut, and he had 22 apiece in consecutive games against Pittsburgh and St. John's. His average for the year was 11.8 points per game, 5.6 assists, and 3.5 rebounds. But those totals tended to run low against teams that were

Tyus Jones works his way through the Virginia defense during Duke's Jan. 31 win over the second-ranked Cavaliers. Jones led Duke with 17 points. His 3-pointer with 11 seconds remaining sealed the victory.

not as challenging; he recorded just three total field goal attempts—and made none—against Furman and Elon. Jones kicked it into overdrive once the conference season started, though.

"I'm just so blessed," he said after helping Duke rally to win in overtime in his first game against North Carolina, registering 22 points, eight assists, and a career-best seven rebounds at Cameron Indoor Stadium. "It's just an honor to wear 'Duke' across my chest, just to represent this program, the tradition of the rivalry."

When Duke lost back-to-back games to North Carolina State and Miami after starting 14-0, Jones was front and center with the changes installed by Mike Krzyzewski and the coaching staff. It was like they gave him the keys to an even better car, one he drove all the way to the Final Four.

Jones was at his best in the national championship game against Wisconsin, as fired up as he'd been for the game in Madison before Christmas. With Jones' old buddies Okafor and Winslow on the bench in foul trouble, Grayson Allen came up big during Duke's comeback against the Badgers. But it was Jones who had the biggest role in helping Duke win its fifth championship. He scored 19 of his 23 points in the second half to spur the comeback. The only other game in which he scored more points was when he fueled another Duke second-half comeback in the regular season finale at Chapel Hill. Yes, he sure knew when to turn it up a notch, drive that car around the curves a little faster.

Jones played 37 minutes in the title game, turned the ball over just once, and hit the three-pointer that put Duke ahead to stay with four minutes remaining. He was named Most Outstanding Player of the Final Four, an award that trumps any national high school award his taller classmates might have received, but to him the MOP is a team award, a reward for the hard work everyone put in. "This has been our one goal that we were working for," he said after the national championship. "No matter if it was getting up extra shots or extra running, trying to get in better shape, tough practices, just believing in one another, believing in coach, everything they were telling us, because we knew at the end if we did accomplish this, it was all going to be worth it." ∎

Tyus Jones goes up for a layup during the first half of the NCAA title game against Wisconsin. Jones was named Most Outstanding Player of the Final Four.

FEBRUARY 7, 2015 • DURHAM, NORTH CAROLINA
DUKE 90, NOTRE DAME 60

ALMOST PERFECT

Blue Devils Avenge Loss, Dominate Irish

By Mike Lopresti

Here is how Justise Winslow described the order of business for Duke's first Saturday in February.

"We wanted to have a great Cameron Indoor moment."

Notre Dame quickly, and painfully, found out what that meant.

With five minutes to go in the first half, it was 40-13.

At one point, the Blue Devils outscored the Irish 43-7.

At halftime, Duke was shooting 81 percent. The final score was 90-60, the worst Notre Dame loss this century.

How to describe that from the winning side?

"Almost perfect," Mike Krzyzewski said.

Or as Amile Jefferson noted, "Everyone was hungry today."

How to describe that from the losing side?

"It was one of those where you're hanging on for dear life," Mike Brey said. Later, he would say that that the thrashing was so total, he had checked the stat sheet to "make sure it only counted as one loss."

And this was the Irish team that had beaten the Blue Devils only 10 days earlier.

Duke's balance was as impressive as its dominance. There had been a theory going around that national player of the year candidate Jahlil Okafor wasn't getting enough help. He had only four points at halftime. His teammates had 46.

"In the locker room, we know this is not a one-dimensional team," Okafor said. "I guess in the first half today, the country got to see that."

At least, Notre Dame did.

Okafor ended with 20, and Winslow 19. Then there was Matt Jones, who averaged 1.8 points a game as a freshman and had hardly been a priority on any scouting reports this season. He scored 17 points against Notre Dame, with three 3-pointers.

Making his mark in the second half, Jahlil Okafor slams home a dunk. Okafor scored 20 points in the win, including 16 in the game's final 20 minutes.

"I'd be lying if I said I wasn't happy right now," he said. "It's like a sigh of relief to be able to feel good about yourself on the offensive end and not be liability."

Playing time is not the easiest thing to get at Duke. Waiting your turn can get lonely and hard. Jones said Krzyzewski has helped by texting him supportive messages after games.

"I'm a product of that, waiting for my chance," Jones said. "My chance is finally here, I think."

Krzyzewski agreed. "His time is here. It's not coming. It's here."

When the Blue Devils weren't scoring at will, they were shutting down an Irish offense noted for its efficiency. On this afternoon, Duke was a monster at both ends.

"To be honest, this is the defense that coach envisioned us playing the whole year," Winslow said. "This type of intensity, shutting down teams with the athletes we have."

A 30-point win over a top-10 opponent is a first-rate way to send the message that a team is coming together. The Blue Devils had seemed wobbly in January. But it wasn't January anymore.

"The last two weeks we've gone through more than anybody," Krzyzewski said. "There's no question our team has grown. We need to go through a lot of experiences and we don't know what those experiences will end up being, because four of our eight guys are freshmen. You have to grow up being in that (situation) or you lose. And you can even lose and still grow up."

March was coming and Duke was certainly growing up. Ask Mike Brey. ∎

Tyus Jones looks down court against Notre Dame. Jones scored 12 points and dished out seven assists in the Blue Devils' win over the No. 10 Fighting Irish.

2 GUARD

QUINN COOK

Senior's Leadership Proved Key to Title Run

By Mike Lopresti

This was a spring day in 2014. Duke had just lost to Mercer in the NCAA Tournament, and Quinn Cook had been called into a meeting with his coach. He entered the room to find Mike Krzyzewski sitting there. And also...Janet Cook, his mother.

"I didn't know my mom was going to be there. She just showed up in Durham," Cook said. Krzyzewski had a message for his soon-to-be senior. He needed more from him. More leadership, more maturity. There were freshmen coming who would require some on-court tutoring. And he wanted Cook's mother there to emphasize the point.

"It was some things I didn't want to hear, but I needed to hear," Cook said. "That's one thing about coach. He doesn't beat around the bush. He was basically telling me I needed

to grow up. That I still had a chance to be the leader of this team."

Flash forward one year. Duke's national championship was only minutes old, and from the microphone was coming one wise observation after another.

On the Blue Devils' focus on defense and rebounding: "It's the little things that count. It counted today."

On the freshmen: "They didn't think they knew it all. They worked. I mean they worked hard. It's great that it paid off in the biggest game of everybody's lives...I'm just thankful they came to Duke."

On the achievement in general. "We are all blessed to be part of this Duke program."

Sounded like a coach. No, sounded like Quinn Cook. The senior. The leader. The straw who stirred Krzyzewski's concoction.

Quinn Cook takes a one-handed shot during Duke's win over N.C. State in the ACC Tournament. Cook led the Blue Devils with 15 points, including two 3-pointers

The four freshmen electrified the Blue Devils and marched them to the trophy podium at the Final Four. But someone had to be in front of the parade.

"We as coaches say these things," Krzyzewski said at one stop along the tournament road. "But when Quinn says them in his own language and his own way, they resonate even better. He's led us to a fabulous season, and hopefully he'll lead us further into this tournament."

Turns out, Cook led them as far as they could go. That was April. "I said 'I'm going to depend on you,'" Krzyzewski mentioned of his pre-season charge to Cook. "He's taken that to the highest level."

But it was January, when Cook helped save Duke.

Those were days of trouble. The Blue Devils lost by 12 points at North Carolina State, and two days later were pounded at home by Miami 90-74. Cameron Indoor Stadium is supposed to be a place of safety—Duke had won 41 home games in a row—but not at that moment.

It was the first time in six years the Blue Devils had lost consecutive regular season games, the first time in 19 years, they been beaten by double digits in back-to-back games. Trouble was in the air, and Krzyzewski

Quinn Cook goes up for a layup against N.C. State during the ACC Tournament quarterfinals.

admitted, "I haven't been able to figure out how to change it."

It was Cook who said, "to hear Cameron like this is not a good feeling."

Something had to be done, and quickly. A trip to Louisville was in four days, and three defeats in a row would qualify as a tailspin. Then where would the Blue Devils be?

Cook knew what to do. He had the team over to his place for some television. No coaches. Just teammates trying to figure it all out, and a senior doing what he remembered promising to do in that room the previous spring with his coach and his mother.

"We let two games get away from us," Cook said. "When you lose two in a row, your confidence can go elsewhere. We had a big game at Louisville that Saturday. I just wanted to make sure the guys' confidence was okay, and just tell everybody we're fine. I just had everybody to my house to watch TV and to just relax and get away from basketball a little bit, and make sure everybody was okay."

The Blue Devils traveled to Louisville and were better than okay. They defended their way to a 63-52 win. The crisis was passed. "That game," Cook said, "really changed our season around."

The course was set for Indianapolis, April 6. By then, the younger Blue Devils spoke of Cook in near reverence. "Since the first day we got there on campus, he's just really took the leadership," Tyus Jones said. "So we've just followed him ever since."

By then, the coach/player bond between Krzyzewski and Cook had been Superglued together. "Along through the season, you just become really close to somebody," Krzyzewski said. "It's like (through) the frequency of contact, intimate situations, tough situations, that a relationship grows. We have an unbelievable relationship."

By then, Cook had a full understanding of how he wanted it all to end. He had listened to Krzyzewski talk about the Blue Devils of the past who had come to own their own March and April.

"We don't get tired of it. We love it when he breaks out into one of his stories," Cook said the day before the national championship game. "You obviously want to be one of those players he talks about in the future."

Oh, he will be. The next night, Krzyzewski and Cook stood together on the podium. Two men who understood their road just taken. ∎

Quinn Cook stretches to the rim against N.C. State during the ACC Tournament. Cook's senior leadership was essential to Duke's 2015 title run.

FEBRUARY 18, 2015 • DURHAM, NORTH CAROLINA
DUKE 92, NORTH CAROLINA 90 (OVERTIME)

AN INSTANT CLASSIC

Blue Devils Outlast Tar Heels in First Matchup Since Dean Smith's Passing

By Matt Silverman

Duke vs. North Carolina is a basketball event matching two tradition-rich programs led by legendary coaches and located just a few miles from each other. And when both schools are ranked in the top 15, a Duke-North Carolina game has the potential to be an instant classic. This was.

Duke didn't win so much as survived. The Blue Devils' 92-90 overtime victory at Cameron Indoor Stadium exhausted the schools, their fans, and even third-party bystanders watching on ESPN. "It's tough for this game to always live up to the hype," Duke coach Mike Krzyzewski said. "But I think tonight's game exceeded it."

The night began with the teams and coaches exchanging hugs. It was the first meeting between the schools since the death of legendary UNC coach Dean Smith less than two weeks earlier. Duke fans showed respect for the man who coached UNC for 37 seasons and beat the Blue Devils 59 times, including a 24-14 record against Krzyzewski. "He was looking down," Coach K said of Dean Smith. "He might not have liked the result of the game, but I'm sure he liked the way both teams played."

Coach Roy Williams' Tar Heels, losers of three of four coming in, had trouble keeping up with Duke in the early going. As Williams put it, "The first four minutes I thought we were brain-dead."

According to the players, both teams were revved for the rivalry game as well as the tribute to Dean Smith. "It was a lot of emotion, a lot of good emotions," said Jahlil Okafor, playing his first game against North Carolina. "We were really hyped tonight, but they were missing a lot of shots and it was a game of runs. We weren't expecting to blow North Carolina out—that's not usually how this rivalry goes, but we definitely got off to a really good start."

Just 4:50 into the game, Duke was ahead,

Quinn Cook drives to the basket against North Carolina. Cook hit five 3-pointers in the first half.

17-6. The Blue Devils shot 58 percent in the half, and the lead reached 13. Captain Quinn Cook put up 15 first-half points—all on 3-pointers. J.P. Tokoto's dunk for North Carolina just before the buzzer made it a seven-point game at intermission.

But the problems came to the fore in the second half. Though UNC tried just 10 3-pointers (making two) and had seven shots blocked—six by Duke junior Amile Jefferson—the Tar Heels worked hard on the inside, scoring 62 points in the paint. The game turned around in the second half, with UNC jumping ahead five minutes in and pushing the lead to 77-67 after Nate Britt's layup through the lane with 3:51 remaining.

No panic set in—and no play was sent in. "It's not like we drew up anything," said Mike Krzyzewski. "When they came back, that was on them. We just said, 'Play. Follow your instincts and play.' And they did."

Tyus Jones' instincts led him to nine straight points. First he fed Justise Winslow (16 points, 7 rebounds) for a 3-pointer, and then—following a Winslow dunk—Jones scored nine points in just over a minute: a layup, two free throws, a jumper inside, a free throw, and finally a game-tying layup with 25 seconds left. North Carolina had the last possession and Marcus Paige took the shot, but the ball bounced off the rim as both teams wrestled in the lane. No fouls were called. Overtime would decide it.

As much effort as both sides put in, an inelegant part of the contest was foul shooting. Duke shot just 51 percent from the foul line, including 3 of 9 in overtime—with four straight misses. The Blue Devils were quite efficient from the field in OT, hitting four of six shots, including two layups by Okafor, each coming after North Carolina went ahead. Quinn Cook, who, like Tyus Jones, scored 22 points, connected on two of four free throws in the final 31.8 seconds of overtime. That wound up being the final margin. North Carolina had two shots to tie the game in the last 5.2 seconds but missed both.

It was a test of stamina. Three Blue Devils played at least 40 minutes: Cook stayed in the entire game, Jones sat just two minutes in the first half, and Okafor (12 points, 13 rebounds) played 41 minutes despite spraining an ankle in the first half.

"Our guys are in really good shape, but I think playing at home helped," Krzyzewski said. "I think our sixth man really helped give us energy. You kind of forget about being tired." ∎

Jahlil Okafor passes the ball in the second half. The freshman center, playing on a sprained ankle, contributed 12 points, 13 rebounds, and three assists in 41 minutes.

MARCH 7, 2015 • CHAPEL HILL, NORTH CAROLINA
DUKE 84, NORTH CAROLINA 77

TAKING TOBACCO ROAD

Duke Freshmen Take Over to Spoil UNC's Senior Day

By Matt Silverman

The final game of the regular season was not the dogfight that the first Duke-North Carolina meeting had been a couple of weeks earlier. But it was no pushover—Tobacco Road rivalry games rarely are.

Like the first meeting, the Tar Heels held a lead well into the second half, but it was Duke's relentless offense—plus a few key turnovers—that resulted in an 84-77 win in the 240th Duke-UNC men's basketball game. All but one of those games, a 1971 NIT Tournament game won by UNC, took place during either the regular season or ACC Tournament, but rivalry games are their own separate category, always filled with meaning regardless of circumstances.

Duke had already locked up its 19th Atlantic Coast Conference regular season title (second only to UNC's 29) and looked very much like a one seed in the NCAA Tournament.

Meanwhile, 19th-ranked North Carolina, barring an ACC Tournament championship run, seemed unlikely to snag a two seed in the NCAA Tournament even if the Tar Heels could finish the schedule by beating the third-ranked team in the country. Yet UNC made the Blue Devils work hard enough that no matter how many of Duke's freshmen might opt for the NBA draft, they would remember their first trip to Dean Smith Center.

One month to the day after Dean Smith died at 83, the legendary UNC coach's presence hung over the proceedings at the building named for him. Duke honored the North Carolina coach synonymous with grace and class when the teams met in Durham in February. So before the rematch at Chapel Hill, UNC honored Duke coach Mike Krzyzewski for surpassing 1,000 career victories. Krzyzewski had already exceeded Smith's previous records of 879 wins and 65

Justise Winslow finds a path to the basket against North Carolina. Battling foul trouble, Winslow scored 13 points in 22 minutes.

NCAA Tournament game victories, among other marks. When the rivals hit the court, however, Krzyzewski's team was a little off.

Duke went more than 10 minutes without a point and shot just 33 percent in the first half, its third-worst shooting half of the year. Only a 7-3 spurt in the last three minutes kept the Blue Devils within a basket at 33-31 at intermission, with 13 points by Quinn Jones. Duke looked sluggish starting out the second half. A three-pointer by UNC's Marcus Paige, who had 17 of his 24 points in the second half, put the Tar Heels up 49-42 with 14:40 remaining. Then Duke's underclassmen took over Senior Day at Chapel Hill.

Tyus Jones fed Jahlil Okafor for a jumper that sparked a 14-2 run. Jones made a pair of free throws, and then hit a lay-in to cut the lead to one. But Jones also hit the basket stanchion and was forced to go to the bench, where Justise Winslow was already sitting with four fouls. With UNC still holding a one-point lead with 12:21 left, sophomore Matt Jones nailed a three-pointer to put the Blue Devils on top. Half a minute later he fed freshman Grayson Allen for a three-pointer and suddenly Duke was ahead by five.

"Matt, he only has one bucket in the game, we're down 51-50 and knocks that thing down," Krzyzewski said. "I love that, that he knows we have enough confidence in him and he has enough confidence in him to take it. One of the cool things with this group—I have a special group of guys. I'm not saying we're a great team, but we have a special group of guys. Those three—Justise [Winslow], Jah [Jahlil Okafor] and Tyus—are on the bench, and they're cheering like crazy for those guys."

Besides cheerleading, Tyus Jones kept busy on the court. Despite back spasms following his collision, he scored 17 of his 24 points in the second half. As ESPN told it, Jones became the first Duke player to have 20 points and seven assists in his first two games against UNC. He also became the first Duke freshman ever to hit all 12 free throws in a game.

When asked about Tyus Jones's talent, Krzyzewski said, "I've seen it from a freshman, like [Tommy] Amaker, [Bobby] Hurley. Okay, that's it. That's where he is. Tyus is outstanding."

North Carolina coach Roy Williams acknowledged the talent on the other side of the court: "I'm tired of saying this, but [congratulations to] Duke." It would not be the last congratulations the Blue Devils would receive in 2015. ∎

Jahlil Okafor puts up a shot against North Carolina. The freshman center scored 14 points, including a key second-half jumper that sparked a 14-2 run.

MARCH 12, 2015 • GREENSBORO, NORTH CAROLINA
DUKE 77, NORTH CAROLINA STATE 53

NO WOLFPACK RERUN

Blue Devils Avenge First 2015 Loss, Cruise to Victory Over In-State Foe

By Matt Silverman

Almost two months to the day before taking on North Carolina State in the ACC tournament quarterfinals, Duke, 14-0 and ranked No. 2 in the country, came to Raleigh and lost its unbeaten status. The 87-75 defeat to the unranked Wolfpack was humbling. "Going in the locker room, feeling like the world had ended," freshman Jahlil Okafor told Sports Illustrated of his first college loss. What the loss actually did was open up a new world for the Blue Devils.

Freed from the pressure of remaining undefeated—or constantly being reminded about it—the Blue Devils could take their place in the polls behind Kentucky and Virginia, and let those two teams field all of the questions about how tough it is to stay undefeated. Duke, meanwhile, could regroup. Even rethink.

Duke lost its next game, at home, against another unranked team—the University of Miami. At that point the coaching staff decided to try something radical for Duke: zone defense. The Blue Devils hit the road, knocked off Rick Pitino's Louisville club, which was ranked sixth in the country at the time. "That game really changed our season around," senior Quinn Cook said. "Guys, our freshmen, our sophomores, Amile [Jefferson], everybody stepped up in a big way." So did the coach. Mike Krzyzewski had always used man-to-man defense, and now with a talented team of freshman guided by the trusted Cook, the Blue Devils could make adjustments on the go.

"If you handle losses the right way, then losses can be very beneficial," Krzyzewski said late in the season. "What you do with a win or a loss determines how much better you are going to be. We've always tried to use the losses as learning experiences and not just punish somebody."

Maybe he should have told NC State that

Duke center Marshall Plumlee finishes a dunk during Duke's ACC Tournament quarterfinals win over North Carolina State. The senior came off the bench to score 12 points on six dunks.

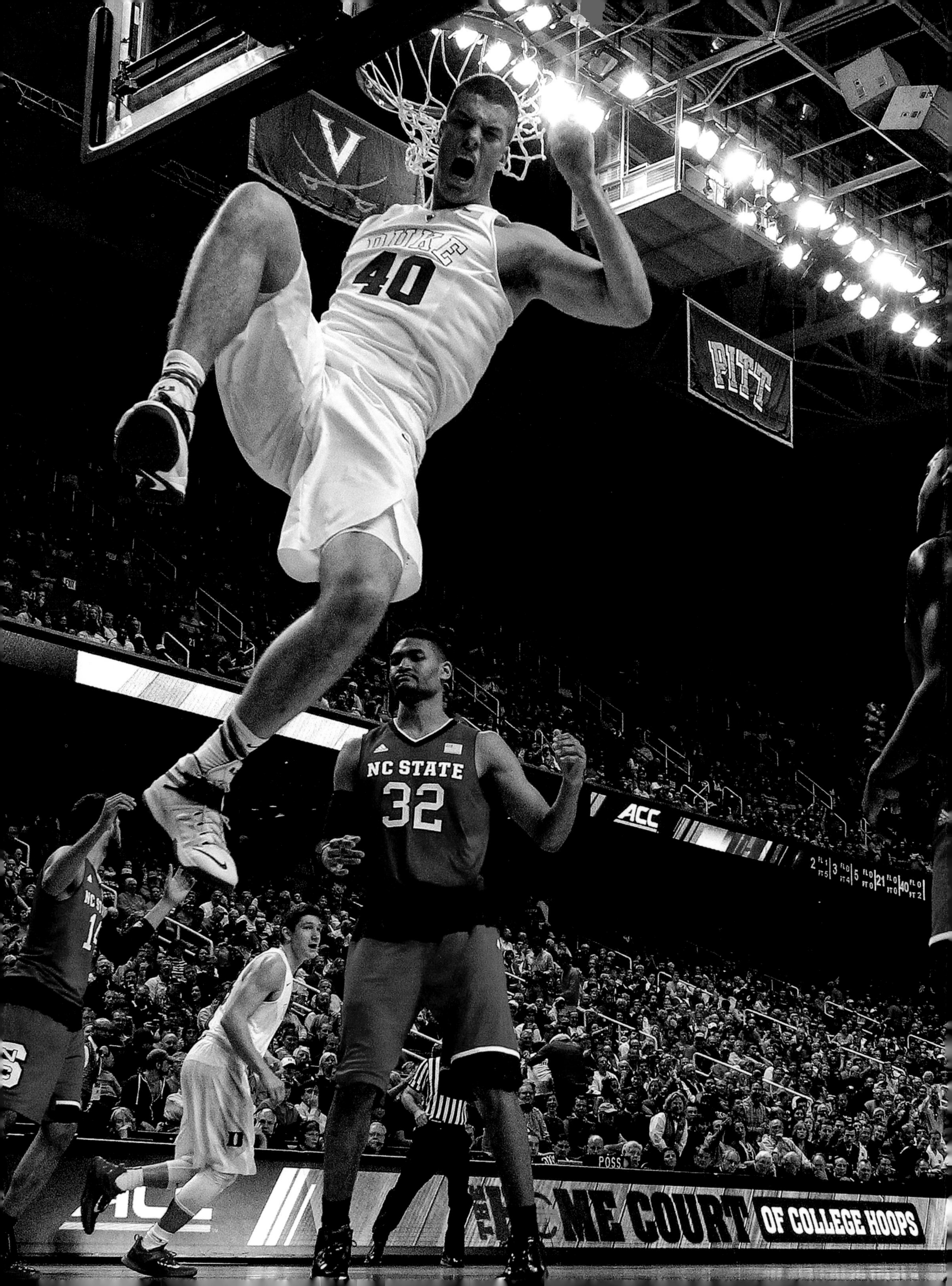
DUKE
40
PITT
NC STATE
32
ACC
ME COURT
OF COLLEGE HOOPS

before the ACC tournament. Duke demolished the team that had ended the Blue Devils' undefeated run in January. The March rematch was a 77-53 pasting. Duke never trailed.

Though the Blue Devils lost three times in January, they did not lose at all in November, December, or February. Despite having reeled off 11 straight wins before their rematch with the Wolfpack in the conference tournament, Krzyzewski installed yet another zone defense: the 1-3-1. Duke doubled NC State's shooting percentage (58 percent to 29), and scored on 22 of its first 26 possessions. Marshall Plumlee had two alley-oop dunks, and his teammates sank shots with hands in their faces, recovered from stumbles to bury treys.

The Blue Devils led 49-22 at intermission—and that was with point guard Tyus Jones not scoring at all in the half (though he did have six assists). Ralston Turner (13 points) was only member of the Wolfpack to have more than one basket in the first half. Five Blue Devils had at least seven points, with Justise Winslow recording 11 points in the first 20 minutes.

The lead reached 30 less than three minutes into the second half. The point had been made, but Duke stayed on point: Six players finished in double figures, 10 players stepped onto the court, the team dished out 14 assists, and Duke committed just five turnovers. They did miss a free throw, but made the other dozen.

Anthony "Cat" Barber, who'd scored 34 points the previous day in N.C. State's victory over Pittsburgh, was held scoreless by Duke and sent to the locker room early after colliding with Amile Jefferson midway through the second half. N.C. State, which had shot 55 percent against Duke in January, shot 35 percent against them in the ACC tournament.

"We played a team defense that required us to talk," explained Marshall Plumlee, whose 12 points—on 6 dunks—was second on the team to Quinn Cook's 15. "And when we're talking, we're a better defensive team. So whenever there is a weak spot in the zone, we talk, we'd compensate, and it was just a lot of movement, a lot of activity."

Zoned in, fired up, chatty, and playing like the number two team in the country—Duke seemed to be peaking at just the right time of the year. ∎

Matt Jones drives to the basket during the ACC Tournament quarterfinals. Jones scored 11 points in the win.

MARCH 13, 2015 • GREENSBORO, NORTH CAROLINA
NOTRE DAME 74, DUKE 64

'AN OUT OF BODY EXPERIENCE'

Irish Jump Out to Huge Lead, Hold On to Beat Blue Devils

By Matt Silverman

Duke's first ACC tournament foe, North Carolina State, had a chance, in theory, but Notre Dame was the only team to beat the 2014-15 Duke Blue Devils twice.

The first came in January, a four-point Notre Dame win that was the third loss in six games for the Blue Devils. Duke was tinkering with its defense and its lineup. The day after the loss in South Bend, junior guard Rasheed Sulaimon (averaging 7.5 points and 2.5 rebounds per game off the bench) was dismissed from the team for being "unable to consistently live up to the standards required to be a member of [the] program."

Duke's second loss to Notre Dame had less off-court drama. The Fighting Irish were able to hang on, 74-64, to earn a spot in the ACC tournament final after finishing 13th in its conference debut a year earlier. The Blue Devils, who did beat Notre Dame by 30 points in Durham in February, came close but could come all the way back from a 17-point deficit.

The Fighting Irish jumped out to a quick lead, doing their damage inside and scoring 16 of their first 17 points in the paint and 30 of their 41 points in the first half from in close. Notre Dame's Bonzie Colson (14 points) and Demetrius Jackson (11) combined for 25 by intermission as the Irish led, 41-26. Kryzyzewski likened his team's out of character sluggishness and lack of communication in the first 24 minutes to "an out of body experience."

Duke freshman Jahlil Okafor scored 15 of his team's 26 points in the first half. He was on a mission following a talk with coach Mike Krzyzewski. "[We] talked before the game and he told me I wasn't playing as well as I needed

Mike Krzyzewski, players, and assistants look on from the Blue Devils bench during the final minutes of Duke's loss to Notre Dame in the ACC Tournament semifinals.

to," Okafor said. "So just trying to play better for my teammates. The past couple of weeks they've really been playing well and that's why we've been winning. So I feel like I let my teammates down. We played with a lot of heart tonight and I tried to get my teammates going. But for March Madness or the next postseason it's the same thing. Just try to be dominant, get my teammates going and try to help them out a little bit."

The second-ranked team in the country determined to get better despite taking a 12-game winning streak into a game against the last team to beat them? That spoke to the team's willingness to continually improve. Coming back from the dead in the ACC tournament semifinal spoke to not giving up on a game.

Duke trailed by 17 but was finally able to cut into Notre Dame's lead late in the second half. Okafor's jumper made it a five-point game with four minutes left, but those would be the last points of his monster day (28 points, eight rebounds). After a pair of foul shots by Notre Dame's Jerian Grant, Quinn Cook came down the floor and missed a 3-pointer, Justise Winslow grabbed the offensive rebound and fed Tyus Jones, who had missed his first four 3-point tries, but nailed one with 3:13 left to make it a 68-64 game. Notre Dame, which had blown an 18-point lead before finally beating Miami the night before, scored the last six

points against Duke to earn a trip to the ACC final, where they topped North Carolina, 90-82. Irish coach Mike Brey, a former Duke assistant coach, considered winning the ACC tournament in just Notre Dame's second year in the conference, "No greater achievement in the history of our program." And Notre Dame's basketball program dates back to 1898.

For their part, the Blue Devils got to rest up for the NCAA tournament, confident that the team would get a No. 1 seed. "We've won 29 games and have been one of the best teams in the country with four freshmen and eight guys," Krzyzewski said. "I like my team. We're ready to go to war in the NCAA tournament, and we'll take what the consequences are of our efforts. And each team is different, each team, each season is different." ∎

Jahlil Okafor leans into Notre Dame's Bonzie Colson. Okafor was the game's leading scorer with 28 points.

MARCH 20, 2015 • CHARLOTTE, NORTH CAROLINA
DUKE 85, ROBERT MORRIS 56

LEARN AND ADVANCE

No Early Exit for Young, Talented Blue Devils
By Mike Lopresti

Duke's long NCAA Tournament ride began against Robert Morris, with echoes from the past, and questions about youth.

The Blue Devils' prospects were promising enough as a No. 1 seed, but then there was the memory of Mercer in 2014. And Lehigh in 2012. "It's a new year, it's a new team, it's a new season," said senior leader Quinn Cook, who had seen both upset tournament evictions up close.

Then there was the matter of four freshmen getting their first dose of March. "I just told them to be themselves," Cook said. "I don't want them thinking a lot, so I kind of let them be themselves and act instinctively."

No problem. Duke hit 12 of its first 15 shots and was on its way to an 85-56 victory. Cook showed the kids how it was done with 22 points, and Jahlil Okafor added 21 in his first tournament appearance.

It was a return to form for Duke, after a disappointing early exit from the ACC Tournament. Not that Mike Krzyzewski had leaned on his team in the days in between. "We weren't going to punish our guys or anything like that," he said. "We didn't want to wear them out, we wanted them to get healthy."

Rather than survive and advance, this was more learn and advance.

Take when Krzyzewski called for veterans Amile Jefferson and Marshall Plumlee early in the game. He was hoping they would set an example for Okafor and Justise Winslow. "Jah, Justise, they weren't talking," Krzyzewski said. "They weren't themselves."

Take early in the second half. Okafor missed an ill-advised reverse dunk, choosing glitz over an easy basket. Out of the game, he came. Message time. "You can't do that. That's the easy message," Krzyzewski said later.

"You know, two points can end your

Matt Jones drives past Robert Morris's Elijah Minnie during the second half. Jones contributed five points and four assists in Duke's convincing win in their NCAA tournament opener.

season," Cook said. "Freshman mistake. Jah knows that and he bounced back from it."

A moment later, Krzyzewski did not like what he saw on the court in focus or approach, so he called a timeout for a brief and pointed lecture.

"You just do it by feel. I know them well enough. I feel like I can get emotional, funny, serious, and they'll respond because of the relationships that are built," he said. "It's my responsibility to spontaneously act when I do have a feel, when I do see something, and for them to react to me. And they've done that, and they did it tonight."

The Blue Devils learned something else, too. Opponents do not just fold up and go away in March. Robert Morris cut a 20-point lead to 10 in two minutes in the second half, until Duke put away the game with a 12-0 run.

In the end, the Blue Devils shot 63 percent and had 28 assists for their 34 field goals. Winslow broke loose for several key plays in the game-clinching run and had 11 rebounds. "'I'm happy I got my first NCAA game out of the way," he said. Five Duke players scored in double figures. Cook had hit six 3-pointers.

All in all, not a bad Friday outing.

"I hope it gives those guys confidence as freshmen, get that good game under their belt," Cook said. "We'll be back on Sunday." ∎

Jahlil Okafor shoots over Robert Morris's Rodney Pryor during the second half. Okafor scored 21 points in the win.

MARCH 22, 2015 • CHARLOTTE, NORTH CAROLINA
DUKE 68, SAN DIEGO STATE 49

ONE STEP CLOSER

Okafor, Cook, and Winslow Lead Blue Devils Past Aztecs

By Mike Lopresti

Two games into the NCAA Tournament, Jahlil Okafor made clear his intentions, both in deed and in words.

First came 26 points to lead Duke past San Diego State 68-49, including 18 in the first half to get the Blue Devils rolling.

Then came his answer to the question on the matter of a national championship.

"It would mean the world to me," he said. "Me, Justise, Tyus, Grayson, the freshmen who came in here, we had one big dream of winning the national title. That's what led me to come to Duke.

"We're putting everything on the line, and that's our No. 1 goal."

He seemed to mean it. Duke shredded one of the nation's better defenses with 54.5 percent shooting. Okafor made 12 of his 16 shots, but as San Diego State coach Steve Fisher noted, "He's not the Lone Ranger." Quinn Cook added 15 points and Justise

Winslow 13, to go with 12 rebounds, five assists, four steals, three blocks—everything but a partridge in a pear tree.

"It takes us to a whole other level," Mike Krzyzewski said of Winslow's game, when it is in full bloom, not to mention Okafor, too. "Those two kids played at a really high level."

So after one weekend, the freshmen seemed entirely at home in the NCAA Tournament.

"As a kid, you grow up wanting to be in that moment, and play on that big stage," Winslow said. Okafor noted of the first game against Robert Morris, "We kind of felt the pressure of that game and learned."

San Diego State was in retreat early, down as many as 18, but managed to cut the lead to seven with 12 minutes left. Cook's 3-pointer ignited an 11-0 Duke run that restored order. The Aztecs, normally difficult to score against, could not stop Duke's attack. "That hasn't happened the way it did tonight," Fisher said.

Guard Quinn Cook leaves his feet to complete a pass against the Aztecs. Cook scored 15 points—including three 3-pointers—in the win.

"They played like a No. 1 seed."

The 19-point margin had a ring to it. The last time Krzyzewski and Fisher—two of the game's venerable coaches—had met in the tournament was the 1992 national championship game, when Duke beat Michigan by 20.

So the Blue Devils moved on to the Sweet 16 with lots of numerical reasons for confidence. They had shot 58.7 percent in their first two tournament games, including nearly 46 percent from the 3-point line. Forty-four of their 64 field goals had come with assists. They had yet to trail in the second half. The freshmen weren't playing like freshmen.

"This is their first time," Krzyzewski said. "And even for the upperclassmen, most of the questions was what you did last year (as in lose to Mercer). So there wasn't a lot of positive vibe about us being in the tournament.

"I thought our guys had fun this week. We didn't pay attention to anything like that, we just played."

Krzyzewski was especially happy to see how the Blue Devils had responded so resolutely when San Diego State narrowed the lead, just as they had done against Robert Morris.

"That's the thing you can't teach. You don't know if they're going to do it, and they did," he said. "I call it tournament pressure, and they handled it really well, twice." ∎

The Blue Devils' bench celebrates after a 3-point basket in the second half of Duke's win over San Diego State.

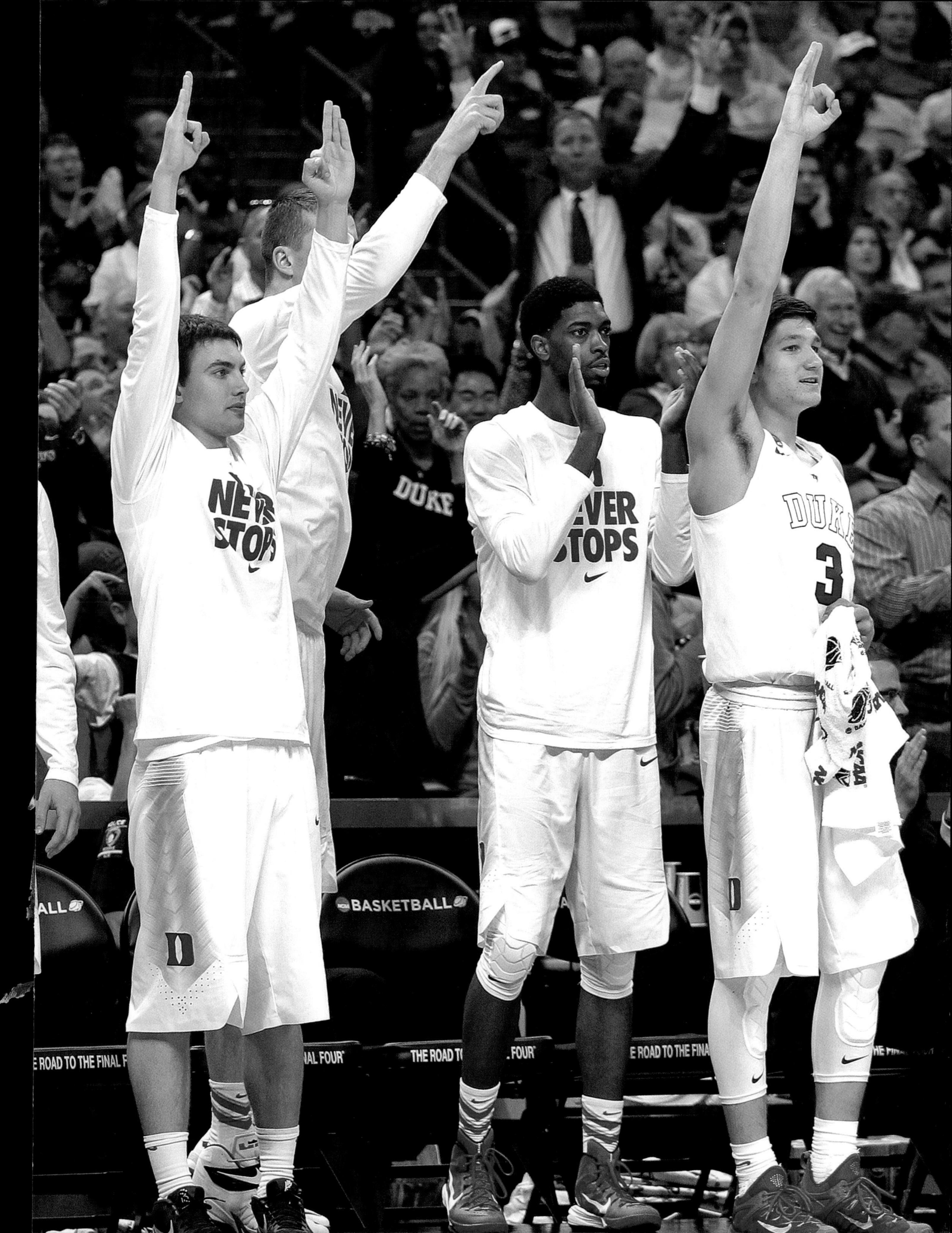
DUKE
STOPS
DUKE
3
BASKETBALL
THE ROAD TO THE FINAL

Jahlil Okafor goes up for a layup against the Aztecs. Okafor led the Blue Devils with 26 points.

"I CALL IT TOURNAMENT PRESSURE, AND THEY HANDLED IT REALLY WELL, TWICE."
—MIKE KRZYZEWSKI

MARCH 27, 2015 • HOUSTON, TEXAS
DUKE 63, UTAH 57

TEXAS JUSTISE

Winslow Shines in Front of Hometown Crowd

By Mike Lopresti

Welcome home, Justise Winslow. Happy birthday, too. The day after he turned 19, Winslow played beyond his years, delivering 21 points and 10 rebounds to push Duke past Utah 63-57 in the South Regional semifinal in Houston.

He didn't look much like a freshman, but then that has been by design.

"Coach never treated us like freshmen," he said of Mike Krzyzewski. "There was never a moment where we felt like freshmen. He gave us his trust and he just believed in us."

To make it even better, Winslow tormented the Utes in his hometown. "I probably knew a hundred people at the game personally. Couldn't give them all tickets. Lot of them had to buy tickets," he said. "It's just really special when you can look out beyond the bench and see your mom and siblings."

Tyus Jones added 15 points, and the Duke defense harassed Utah into 35 percent shooting. That was enough to make it hard to notice Jahlil Okafor scored only six points. But any successful journey through the NCAA Tournament needs a Plan B or Plan C, and someone else to step up. "That's what makes Duke, you know, Duke," Utah coach Larry Krystkowiak said.

It wasn't exactly an offensive tour de force early. Utah didn't score the first 4 ½ minutes of the game, and was still behind only 3-0. But the Blue Devils began to work their way through the Utes defense to lead by as many as 15. "That's what my team has done this year," Krzyzewski said. "They've been able to adapt while the game is going on."

Plus, they made it tough for Utah to score. By the third game of the tournament, defense was steadily becoming a Duke feature.

"They've gotten a bum rap really for not being able to play defense," Krzyzewski said.

Quinn Cook drives to the basket against Utah. Cook scored 11 points as the Blue Devils topped the Utes to advance the Elite Eight.

"We wouldn't win over 30 games unless we're playing good defense.

"We need for Jahlil to score more than six points. That's where the defense has to come in."

It was another example of Duke growth, Duke maturation, Duke development. Eight guys finding ways to win. All reasons why Krzyzewski had become so excited about this team, and this season.

"These guys want to be in the gym. You don't have to twist their arm," he said. "We've cut down our practice like crazy. Never over the last two months have we practiced over an hour in a day. But then the individual work, they might be in there for another hour. They're all really good kids who want to get better and they're easy to coach. They're enthusiastic learners, which makes you a more enthusiastic coach."

The Utes closed in at the end, cutting the lead to 49-43 with the clock just inside of four minutes, Duke needed a big basket.

Winslow, of course, with a jumper. His night, his town.

"He was the best player on the floor," Okafor said. "Maybe because he's in Houston, or maybe because he's 19 now."

Krystkowiak concurred. "Him coming back to Houston, day after his birthday, only juiced up and ready to go. We didn't have an answer." ∎

Mike Krzyzewski calls in a play from the sideline as Utah coach Larry Krystkowiak looks on. In a defensive battle, Duke held Utah to 35 percent shooting.

Justise Winslow puts up a shot past defending Utah forward Jakob Poetl. Playing in his hometown on his birthday, Winslow scored 21 points and grabbed 10 rebounds.

MARCH 29, 2015 • HOUSTON, TEXAS
DUKE 66, GONZAGA 52

A RARE CHALLENGE

Second-Half Comeback Pushes Blue Devils to Coach K's 12th Final Four

By Mike Lopresti

John Wooden. What college basketball coach would not be honored to have a reason to be included in the same paragraph?

"I'm in this moment," Mike Krzyzewski said the day Duke beat Gonzaga 66-52 to win the South Regional and take him to his 12th Final Four, a feat matched only by Wooden. "My past is not important right now."

The moment in Houston was pretty good for Duke. From Tyus Jones providing big shots and assists to be named Most Outstanding Player of the region, to Justise Winslow scoring 16 points in his hometown, to Quinn Cook's leadership—the Blue Devils went marching to the Final Four.

"We've been through some tough times and that made us stronger," Cook said. "I'm just blessed to be a part of Duke.

"I just want to lead these guys with all my heart."

It wasn't easy, but then, going to the Final Four isn't supposed to be. Gonzaga, trying hard to win a first regional championship, pushed ahead 38-34 with 16:20 left. It was a rare challenge to the Blue Devils, who had not been behind like that in the second half the entire tournament.

"You can't hang your head or worry about it," Jones said. "You got to move on to the next play."

The lead didn't last long, but the Bulldogs could not be shaken. They would have tied at 53-53 with under five minutes left, had not Kyle Wiltjer missed an open layup. "He would make that thing 499 times out of 500," coach Mark Few said. "When that happens, just kind of shake your head, and it's not your night."

They were still within range as the clock slipped under three minutes, down 57-51, when Winslow buried a 3-point dagger. He had come home to Houston and enjoyed a splendid weekend.

"Justise is a very special young man, not just a special basketball player," Krzyzewski said.

Tyus Jones attempts a floater. Jones, who was named Most Outstanding Player of the regional, contributed 15 points and six assists in the win over Gonzaga.

On the day its Final Four hopes were on the line, Duke committed three turnovers the entire game. When Gonzaga was beginning to believe in an upset, the Blue Devils allowed the Bulldogs 14 points in the final 16 minutes. "Spectacular, not good," Krzyzewski called the defense.

For Cook, down to his last chance to get to a Final Four, it was a far different feeling than one year earlier, when the Blue Devils were one and done against Mercer.

"I wasn't really thinking about the past," he said. "I was thinking about this year and a new team."

Same for Krzyzewski, who was not interested in talking about going to 12 Final Fours in his career, but rather going to one in 2015.

"We have eight guys. Four are freshmen," he said. "It's the youngest team I've ever had. No one would ever say that because we're Duke, or because it's me. There are eight guys. There's not somebody hiding in the locker room that's going to come out and appear.

"I'm not saying this because we've won, I've said it the whole year. I love my team. They are a pleasure to be with, and as a result, they're taking me to Indy, which is kind of neat."

Not to mention kind of a good omen. Krzyzewski had been to two previous Final Fours in Indianapolis. Duke won them both. ∎

Mike Krzyzewski holds the net after Duke's win over Gonzaga. The win secured Duke's 12th trip to the Final Four under Coach K, tying John Wooden's record.

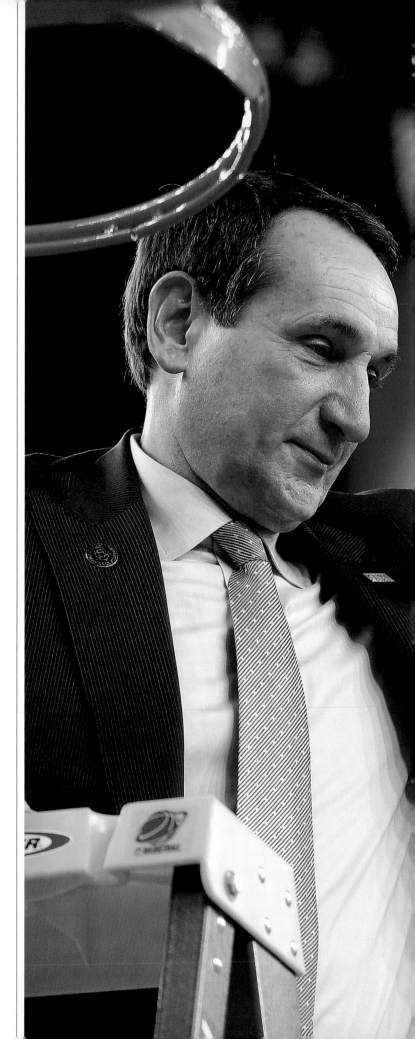

Duke's Justise Winslow extends for a layup against Gonzaga. Playing in his hometown, Winslow scored 16 points.

Duke's Blue Devil mascot and head coach Mike
Krzyzewski take in the action during Duke's Sweet
16 game against Utah in Houston.